Claire Llewellyn

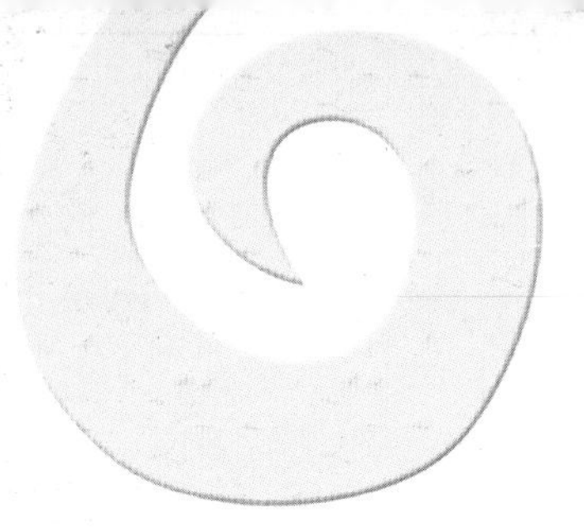

Contents

Chapter 1

All About Hair

We all have hair. It grows longer every day. The hair on our head grows about 15 centimetres in a year. We have about one million hairs on our head.

Hair grows out of our skin. It grows faster on warm days. It grows faster when we sleep. Old hairs fall out after about three years, but new ones grow all the time.

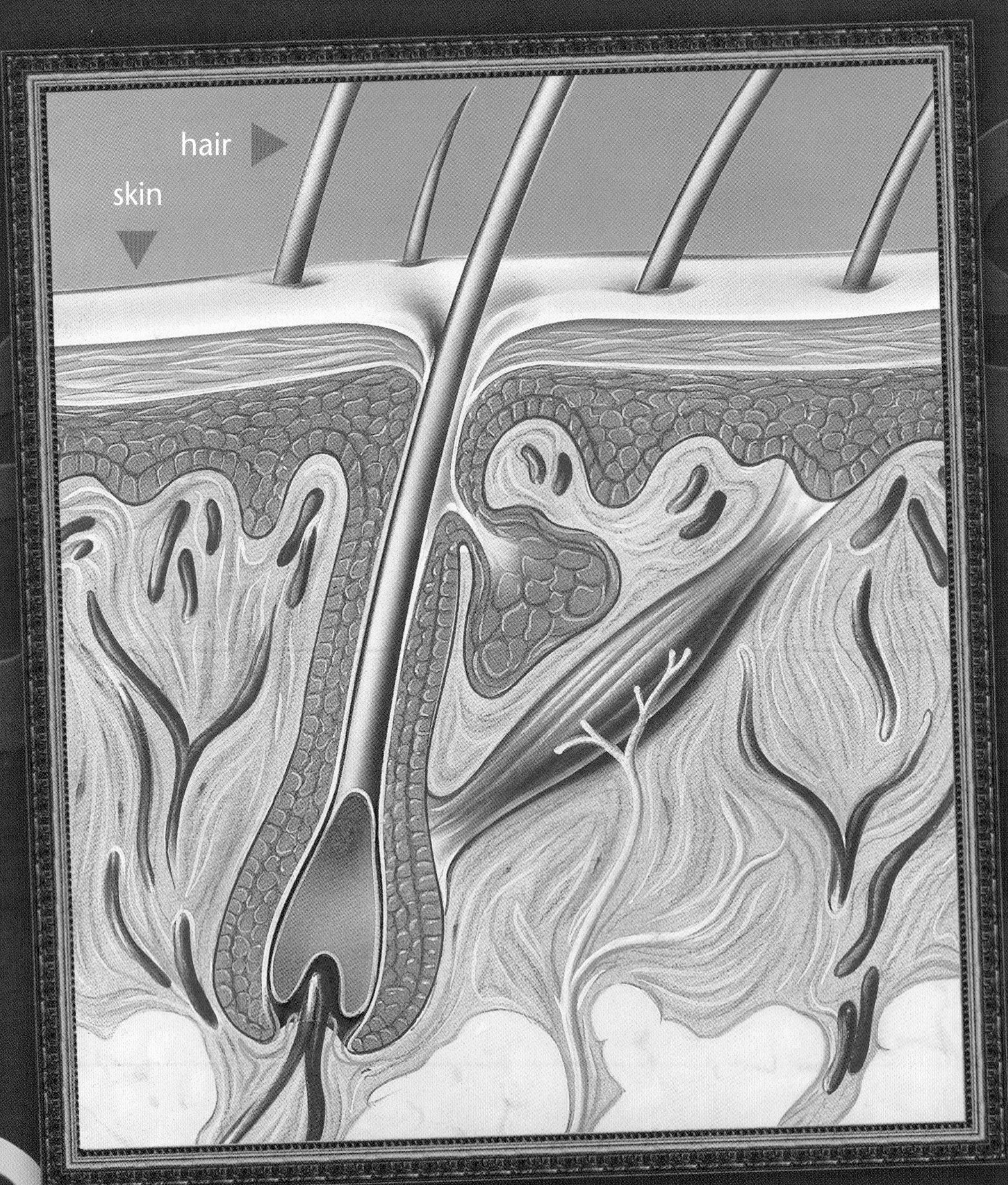

As we get older, our hair can change colour. It can also fall out forever. Many older men lose some of their hair. Sometimes they go bald.

At age 1, Peter had blond hair.

At age 29, he had brown hair.

At age 42, he began to lose his hair!

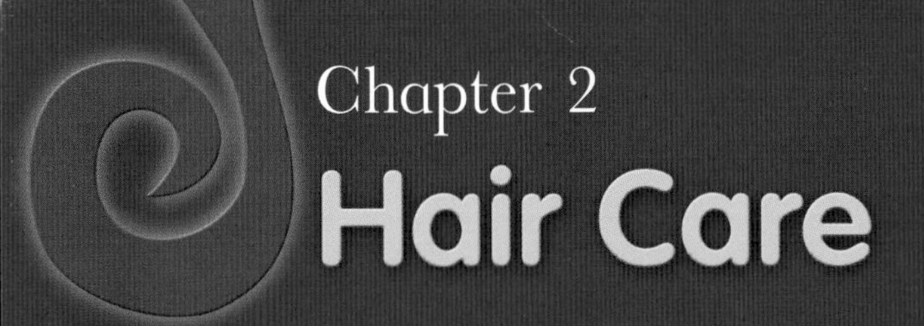

Chapter 2
Hair Care

We take care of our hair. The Romans, who lived 2,000 years ago, took care of their hair too. They brushed and combed their hair often. But they washed it only once a year!

Today, we brush and comb our hair every day. We also wash our hair often. We use many things to help make our hair look nice.

Many people cut their hair to stop it getting too long. About 150 years ago, men and boys had their hair cut by barbers. Everyone had the same haircut then. It was short at the back and sides.

Today, many men and women get their hair cut by a hairdresser. Hairdressers wash and cut hair. They colour, curl and style hair too. But there are still barbers who cut and style hair for men and boys!

Chapter 3

Hairstyles

Hair can be worn in all kinds of styles. About 250 years ago, people wore very big hairstyles. Women put flowers, fruit and even birds in their hair. Sometimes the hairstyles were so big that people had to sleep sitting up!

Today, people have many different hairstyles. Some people keep their hair short. Other people let their hair grow long.

Some people have straight hair. Other people's hair is curly. Long ago, women in Egypt often curled their hair. They put mud all over their hair. Then they wrapped it around sticks. When they took the sticks out, their hair was curly.

People with straight hair can still make it curly. Today, they use heated curlers and curling rods. People with curly hair can also make their hair straight!

It is fun to change our hair colour. People have done it for a long, long time. About 200 years ago, many people put powder on their hair to make it look white.

Today, many people colour their hair. Some people use colours like black and brown and blond. Other people use brighter colours like red or green!

People sometimes wear hair that's not their own. This hair is called a wig. Long ago, in hot places, some people wore wigs to keep the sun off their head. These wigs were made of human hair. They were mainly black.

Today, some people wear a wig if they have lost their hair. They also wear them just to look different. Wigs help us to look like someone else!

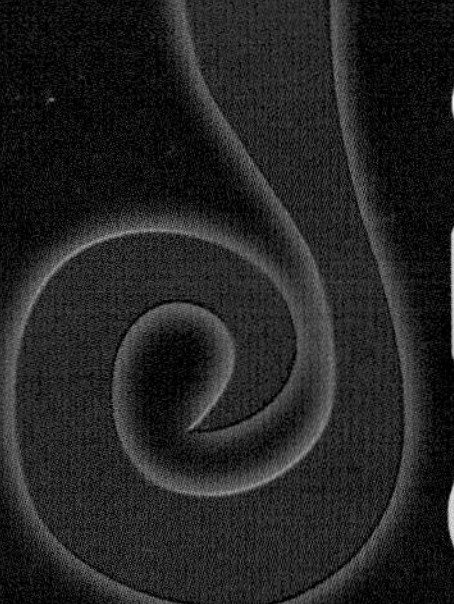

Chapter 4

Hair Today, Gone Tomorrow

Hair grows on men's faces as well as on their heads. Some men let their face hair grow. Some even grow a moustache. About 150 years ago, men had a special tool to keep their moustache dry. It was called a moustache guard.

THE ACME
MUSTACHE GUARD.
Solid Comfort while Eating.
No Use for Napkins.
Neat and simple, easily and quickly adjusted. Does not interfere with free use of mouth.
WORKS PERFECTLY.
Made of gold and silver plate. Can be carried in vest pocket. Every genteel person should have one. Two sizes, large and medium. Mention size when ordering. Price $2.00. Sent by mail to any address. Sold only by the
Acme Novelty Co.,
Omaha, Neb.

Today, many men get rid of the hair on their face. They shave it off with a razor. The first razors were made more than 4,000 years ago. Today, many razors are electric.

Many women pluck the hair in their eyebrows. About 70 years ago, women plucked all the hair from their eyebrows. Then they painted eyebrows on. Are these eyebrows real or painted on?

Today, many women do not want thick eyebrows. To make their eyebrows thin, they pluck some of their eyebrow hairs.

Hair-Raising Facts

Little animals called head lice sometimes live in hair.

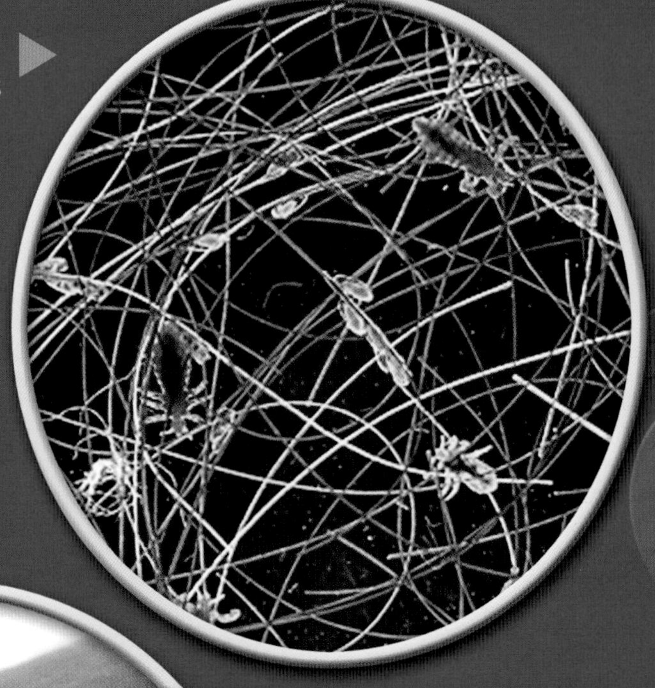

Hair is made of the same stuff as fingernails.

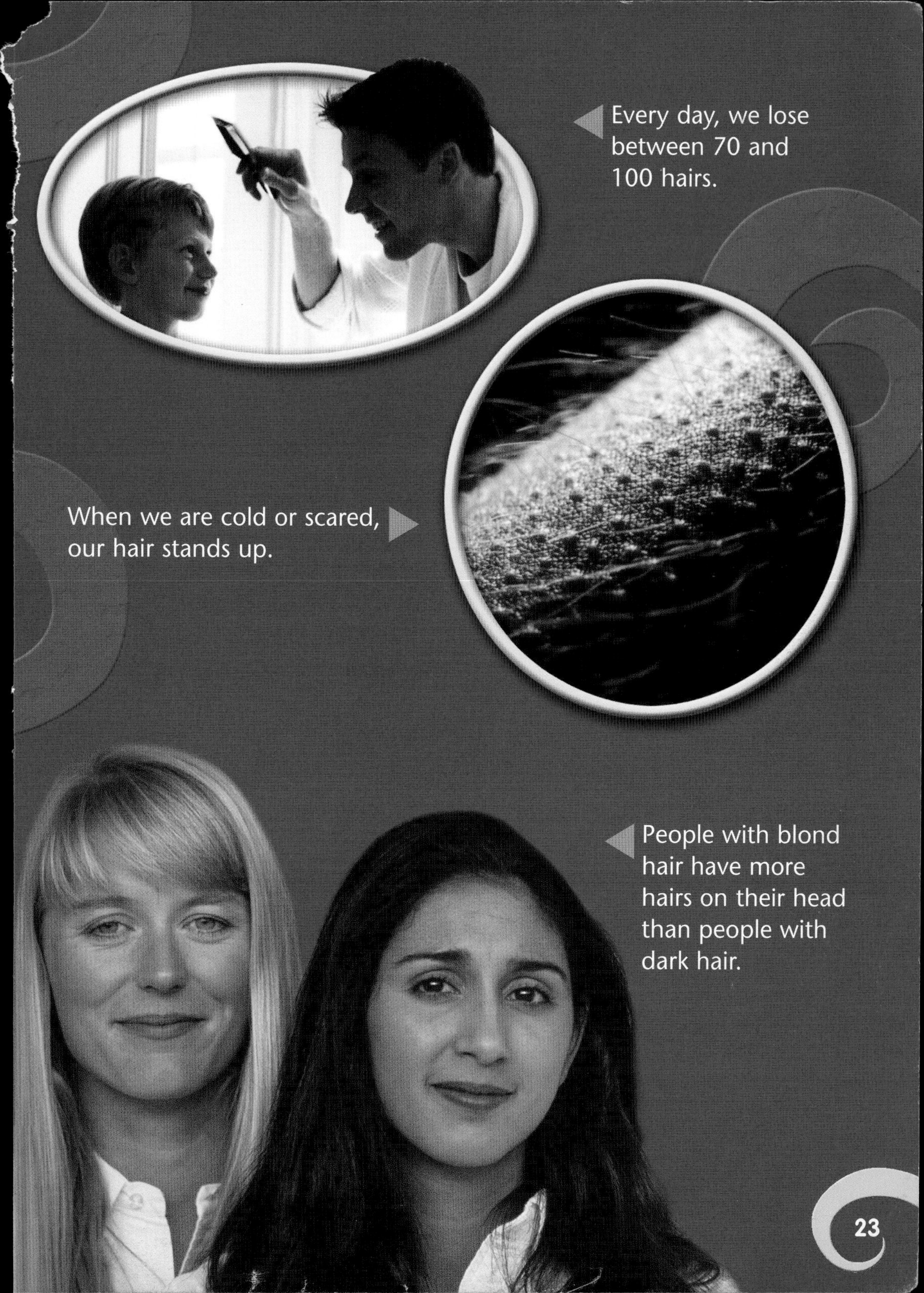

Every day, we lose between 70 and 100 hairs.

When we are cold or scared, our hair stands up.

People with blond hair have more hairs on their head than people with dark hair.

Index